THIS WALKER BOOK

BELONGS TO:

. . . .

. . . .

for
Alexander

First published 1988 by Walker Books Ltd
87 Vauxhall Walk, London SE11 5HJ

This edition published 2008

2 4 6 8 10 9 7 5 3 1

© 1988, 2008 Charlotte Voake

The right of Charlotte Voake to be identified
as author/illustrator of this work has been asserted by her in
accordance with the Copyright, Designs and Patents Act 1988

This book has been handlettered by Charlotte Voake.

Printed in China

British Library Cataloguing in Publication Data: a catalogue
record for this book is available from the British Library

ISBN 978-1-4063-1272-0

www.walkerbooks.co.uk

FIRST THINGS FIRST

Charlotte Voake

WALKER BOOKS

AND SUBSIDIARIES

LONDON • BOSTON • SYDNEY • AUCKLAND

Aa CON

Sit, crawl, stand .... 8 and 9

THE ALPHABET .... 10 and 11

and Great A, Little a 12

Tommy Snooks and Bessy Brooks 13

and DAYS of the WEEK .... 14 and 15

One, two, three, four, five, Once I caught
a fish alive 16

and SOME FISHES 17

NUMBERS .... 18 and 19

One Cat 20

One Dog 21

TENTS

SOME ANIMALS . . . . 22 and 23

Two Cows . . . . 24 and 25

COLOURED RIBBONS . . . . . 26 and 27

Cars and Boats and Planes . . . . 28 and 29

THREE SHAPES 30

and Round About, round about Gooseberry pie 31

SOME FRUIT . . . . 32 and 33

and LOTS OF INSECTS . . . . . . 34 and 35

A CAULIFLOWER, and SOME PEAS 36

Pease Pudding Hot 37

Ring-a-ring o'roses . . . . 38 and 39

and FLOWERS . . . . 40 and 41

BIRDS 42, 43, 44

Zz

Sit

Crawl

Stand

Walk

Run

Jump

Listen

Shout

Touch

Look

Smell

Eat

9

a · b · c · d · e · f · g · h · i · j · k · l · m · n

a b c d e f

n o p q r s t

o · p · q · r · s · t · u · v · w · x · y · z

g h i j k l m

u v w x y z

N · O · P · Q · R · S · T · U · V · W · X · Y · Z

AS Tommy Snooks
And Bessy Brooks
Went walking out
On Sunday,
Said Tommy Snooks
To Bessy Brooks,
"Tomorrow will be Monday!"

MONDAY

TUESDAY

FRIDAY

SATURDAY

ONE, Two, three, four, five,
  Once I caught a fish alive,

Six, seven, eight, nine, ten,
  Then I let it go again.

Why did you let it go?
  Because it bit my finger so.
Which finger did it bite?
  This little finger on the right.

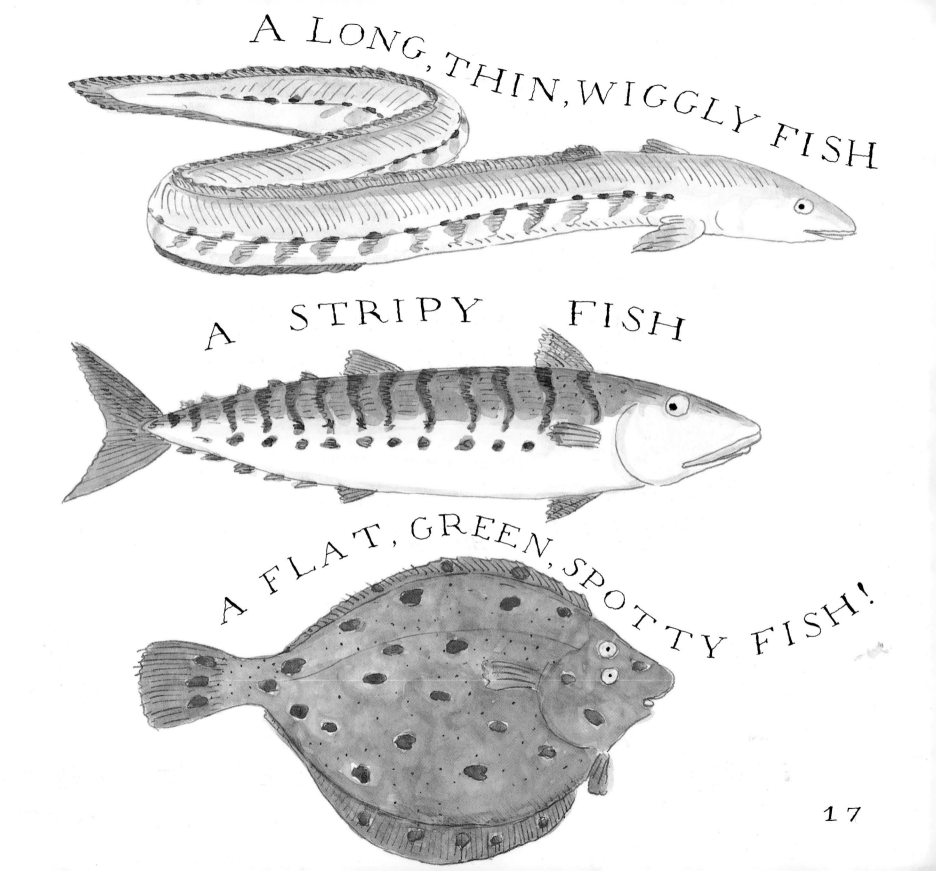

A LONG, THIN, WIGGLY FISH

A STRIPY FISH

A FLAT, GREEN, SPOTTY FISH!

17

ONE CAT

HERE Am I, little Jumping Joan,
When nobody's with me,
I'm always alone.

ONE DOG

BOW Wow wow
Whose dog art thou?
Little Tom Tinker's dog,
Bow wow wow

Squirrel

SOME

LION

Mouse   Rat

Panda   POLAR BEAR   Kangaroos

22

ANIMALS

TIGER

Rabbits

Horse

CAMEL

Elephant

TWO

THE Friendly cow all red and white
  I love with all my heart;
She gives me cream with all her might,
  To eat with apple tart.

Robert Louis Stevenson

COWS

I Never saw a purple cow,
I never hope to see one;
But I can tell you anyhow,
I'd rather see than be one!

Gelett Burgess

COLOURED

PURPLE

RED

RIBBONS

ORANGE

Black

BLUE

YELLOW

PINK

BROWN

GREEN

27

Red  truck

Grey plane

Brown
trailer

28

Green tractor

Pink car

Blue train

Yellow boat

Black
bike

29

THREE SHAPES

triangle

square

circle

ROUND About, round about,
   Gooseberry pie,
My father loves pie,
   And so do I !

SOME FRUIT

Tinker Tailor Soldier Sailor Rich Man

CHERRIES

Poor Man

Thief Beggar Man

Strawberry Banana

PEAR

APPLE

and...

Lacewing

Housefly

LOTS OF

Daddy Long Legs

Grasshopper

Moths

Bee

Ladybird

Earwig

Ants

34

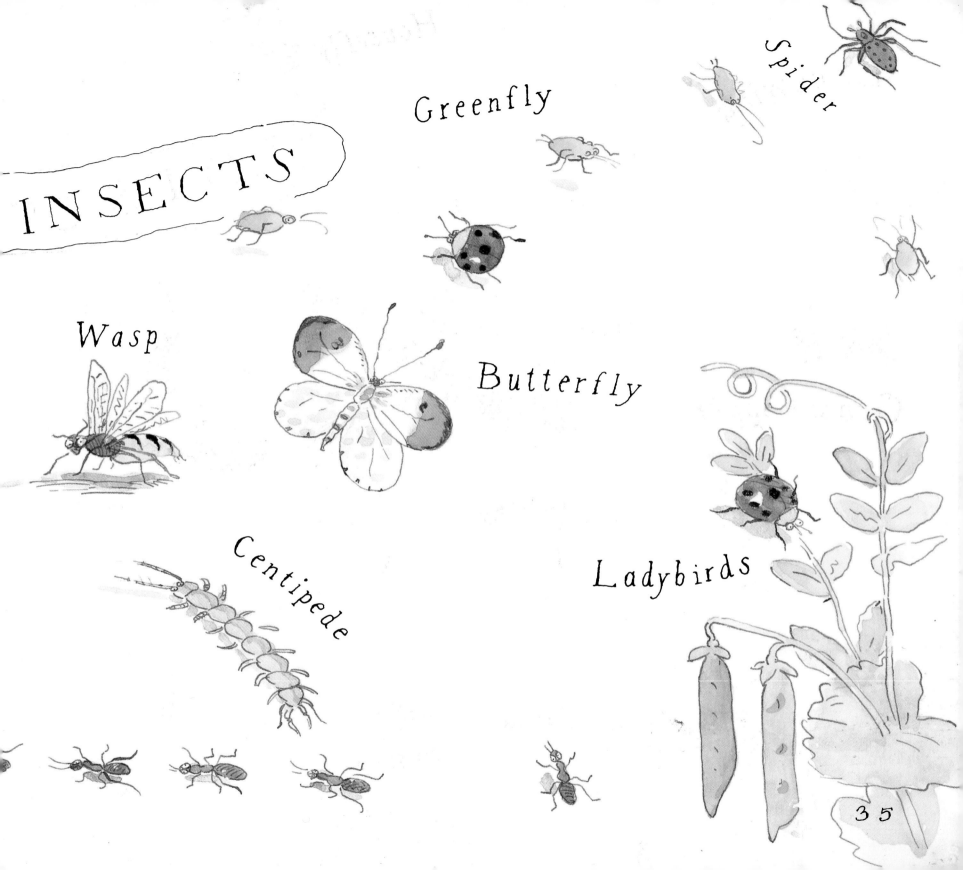

Spider

Greenfly

INSECTS

Wasp

Butterfly

Ladybirds

Centipede

35

A GREAT BIG

CAULIFLOWER

And some LITTLE TINY Peas.

PEASE Pudding hot,
Pease pudding cold,
Pease pudding in the pot,
Nine days old!

Ring-a-ring o' roses,
A Pocket full of posies,

Violet

Daffodil

Dandelion

40

ERS

Buttercup

Shepherd's
Purse

Daisy

41

A DUCK and

A DRAKE

Quack!

And some other birds...

TWO MAGPIES   A Robin

A GOOSE

A Hen

A Blackbird

TU-Whit, tu-whoo,
Goodnight to you!

THE
END

Charlotte Voake

The work of Charlotte Voake is renowned throughout the world for its gentle wit, quiet observation, airy exuberance, and charm. Winner of the **Smarties Book Prize** for *Ginger*, Charlotte says of her work, *"I just draw with ink, over and over again – until I think, 'Aha, that's how it should be!'"*

ISBN 978-1-4063-1269-0

ISBN 978-1-4063-1270-6

ISBN 978-1-4063-1271-3

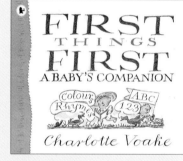

ISBN 978-1-4063-1272-0

ISBN 978-1-4063-0714-6

ISBN 978-1-4063-0523-4

ISBN 978-0-7445-8958-0

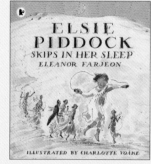

ISBN 978-1-4063-1405-2

Available from all good bookstores

www.walkerbooks.co.uk